GET OUT OF

YOUR OWN WAY

To Susan,

Be wildly successful!

Jovith Jenkins

" 12/11/19 "

GET OUT OF

YOUR OWN WAY

CREATE THE NEXT CHAPTER OF YOUR LIFE

Jovita Jenkins, MBA

Ajides Publishing • Culver City, CA

Jenkins, Jovita.
Get out of your own way : Create the next chapter of your life / Jovita Jenkins – 1st ed.
p. cm.
Includes biographical references.

ISBN 0-9749887-0-7

Dedication

This book is dedicated:

To everyone who dares to get out of their own way, pursue their dreams, and live a life they love.

To my wonderful husband, Akbar, who inspires me to walk through my fears and live my dreams.

To my mother, the fabulous Dottie B., who gave me the gift of believing that I can do anything I set my mind to.

To my darling daughter, Shannita, who grew up to be a marvelous, creative, loving person.

To my faithful friends JoAnn and Joyce.

To my mastermind ladies Dr. Jo, Linda, and Shaune.

To everyone who encouraged or helped me on my journey to recreate my life at midlife.

Table of Contents

Acknowledgments

Completing this book marks a major milestone on my journey to create the next chapter of my life. Like many authors before me, intuitively I knew, deep in my being, that the writer in me would some day emerge. For me, some day has finally arrived. The bottle has been uncorked, and the genie unleashed.

There are so many people who deserve acknowledgment for their support and encouragement as I completed this, the first of many, book writing projects. The list could fill a book. My apologies in advance to those who deserve special recognition who have not been recognized here. I am deeply grateful to each and every one of you for your support.

First, I acknowledge my family, starting with my wonderful husband, Akbar. His love and faith in me has been the wind beneath my wings for the last twenty years. Next, there is my daughter Shannita. I am so proud of her. She leads my promotion team, and is responsible for production of this book. I'd also like to acknowledge my parents, particularly my Mom, the fabulous Miss

Dottie B., who taught me that I could be and do anything I set my mind to. I credit her with instilling in me the courage to pursue my dream of becoming an engineer when peers and teachers tried to convince me that my lot in life was to be a secretary. I am forever grateful.

Supporters who deserve recognition include: Joyce Haynes, who does her best to keep me organized. I must admit, she has a tough job. Joyce is a dear friend and my family has effectively adopted her. Thanks Joyce, I don't know what I would do without you. Next, there are my friends JoAnn and LaVerne, the closest I have ever come to having sisters.

Rounding out my A-list of supporters are my Dream Team and my Mastermind Group. My dream team consists of my husband, Akbar, my daughter, Shannita, and my friend, Joyce mentioned above. The Dream Team also includes Theresa, my web designer, James whose company hosts my websites, and Nancy, my CPA. The Mastermind Group ladies are Dr. Jo, Linda, and Shaune. We support each others' goals and dreams and keep each other accountable for working our plans to turn our individual dreams into reality.

Acknowledgements are appropriate for everyone who influenced my transition from corporate citizen to entrepreneur. Thanks to Fran and company at the Academy for Coach Training, for introducing me to professional coaching. I found coaching at a time in my life when I knew in my heart that it was time for me to reinvent myself and move on to the next chapter of my life. Coaching executives is a passion of mine. It not only gives me the opportunity to help my clients reach their goals, but also gives me the opportunity to affect change at the highest levels of corporate America. Thanks to all of my coaching clients for trusting me with your goals and dreams. It is such a pleasure to watch you work through your issues and find your unique truths based on your own internal wisdom. I am honored to be a part of your discovery process.

Thanks to all the readers of my newsletter who regularly share their thoughts with me via email.

Thanks to each of you who bought this book and use my strategies and tools to aid in your personal transformations.

Last, but by no means least, I thank God for all my blessings.

Introduction

What would you dare to dream if you knew it would come true? What would happen if you could program yourself to be as successful as you would like to be in all areas of your life -- business, career, relationships, health, wealth, and anything else you can think of? What could you achieve if you could just Get Out Of Your Own Way™?

These are questions I have wrestled with for many years, personally, working with colleagues and direct reports in corporations, and with my consulting and coaching clients. We all have a tendency to undervalue our potential. We get stuck between yesterday's commitments and tomorrow's promise. We become so overwhelmed by the events of daily living that if we even remember our grand plan for our lives, we just stop striving to achieve it.

The well-meaning influences in our lives conspire to convince us that the realistic thing to do is to stay where we are and continue to do what we have been doing. What's worse is that we convince ourselves to stay in our safe, familiar comfort zone (rut) even when we know, intuitively, that it is in our best interest to break out and try something new, something that makes our souls sing, that gives our lives purpose and meaning.

This book is for those of you, who like me, are on a quest -- a quest to create a more compelling future. According to Webster's Dictionary, one definition of the word compelling is irresistible. My vision of the ideal compelling future is one where I am doing work I love, with people I respect (and maybe even like). It's making a contribution that leaves the world a little better off because I was in it. My compelling future is not all about work. It includes having meaningful, loving relationships with my spouse, family members, and friends. It's living in a place I love with people I love and who love me in return. It includes at least occasionally having fun (what a concept!). Does this vision appeal to you? How would you like to create and implement a similar vision for yourself? What constitutes your compelling (irresistible) future?

You can accomplish anything your heart desires. You can reinvigorate and reinvent yourself. You have the power within you to start right now to change your life. But first, you must change your thinking about your possibilities and your life. The key is to learn the secret of how to Get Out Of Your Own Way™ and stop blocking your success. My purpose in writing this book is to help you do just that -- Get Out Of Your Own Way™ -- so that you too can create your own compelling future.

What does it mean to Get Out Of Your Own Way™? It means changing beliefs and behaviors that no longer serve you. It means discovering and living your passion and purpose. It means setting goals and taking action toward reaching them. It means overcoming the fear that can hold you back. It means giving yourself permission to dream big dreams and then taking the actions required to turn your dreams into reality.

Using Jovita's Success Prescription described herein, you can begin to think differently about your prospects, your opportunities, your relationships, and your life. While I can't guarantee your success, I can provide tools and strategies to help you significantly increase the odds of making positive, lasting changes in your life. Change can be scary, and uncomfortable. It may seem more comfortable to maintain the status quo. But, if you keep doing what you have always done, you will keep getting the same results that you have always gotten. Creating an irresistible future requires action.

It's time to make a change. Dream big dreams. Develop and implement a plan to turn your dreams into reality. Consistently take actions that move you in the direction of your goals. Get out of your comfort zone. Need help? Keep reading!

Rationale for writing *Get Out Of Your Own Way*™

This book is for anyone who feels stuck and unable to turn their dreams into reality. It is also for anyone who has been overtaken by the realities of living a life that no longer brings them the fulfillment they expected. And, it is for those who want to take an already fulfilling life to the next level. There is something here for anyone who is on a quest to create a more compelling future.

My goal in writing this book is to share wisdom and experience gained over the past half century. After successfully reinventing myself, trading my corporate executive hat for an entrepreneurial one, I felt the desire to give back. My coaching clients and speaking audiences consistently questioned me about my success strategies.

This work was initially envisioned to help those facing dilemmas similar to the ones that I have faced in my life. However, my strategies can be adapted to any number of personal situations.

A major turning point in my life occurred when I realized that the career that I had worked so hard to build, and that I at one time loved so much, no longer suited the person I had become. I was unhappy and frustrated. I decided that my future well-being required that I reinvent myself, again. A very scary thought, particularly since this situation occurred at the height of my no longer fulfilling career as an aerospace executive.

Mine is a story of success against the odds. I completed college while working full time as a secretary and raising my daughter as a single parent. After graduation, with my new degree in Mathematics in hand, I entered the professional workforce as an engineer – the first black woman on Rockwell International's technical staff.

From this jumping off point, I moved on and climbed the corporate ladder. By the end my 30-year career in the aerospace industry, I had helped to shove the glass ceiling up considerably, rising through the ranks to become a successful aerospace executive! Along the way, I met and married by wonderful husband. We shared our 20th wedding anniversary this past December.

Be careful what you ask for. You just might get it. And, you may find it's not what you want or need. The life of an executive was not what I had envisioned. Outwardly, I had all the trappings of success. Inwardly, I knew that it was time for me to find a way to feel more fulfilled. It was time to reinvent myself! In spite of my fears, I embarked on a quest to create a more compelling, irresistible future. Leaving the corporate world behind, I embarked on a new adventure, as an author, speaker, executive coach, and business owner. Consider your life. What is your dream? Are you living it? If not, what are you doing to make it happen?

PART I

The sting of change is nothing compared to the pain of obsolescence.
                    --Unknown

CHAPTER ONE

A Journey Ends

Some people dream of great accomplishments, while others stay awake and achieve them.
                                                    - Unknown

I t was a cold, dreary, stormy afternoon in December. The rain was falling harder than it had in years. As the rain poured down, I watched from a second floor window as the last bus pulled away from the building. It was filled with colleagues from the company I had been a part of for the past quarter century. The expressions on the faces of the people entering that bus can only be described as sad, fearful, and resigned. The unthinkable had happened. After 101 years in business, the company had been acquired in a hostile takeover. Like it or not, TRW no longer existed. The buses were bound for the location of the big tent meeting -- the first encounter with the new company owners.

Watching this scene, through a window from a warm, dry room on the second floor, I knew my decision to leave was the correct one for me. I chose not to attend the tent meeting. It was my last week on the job before retiring. For me, the mandatory employee meeting was optional. Until this moment, I had second-guessed my decision to leave. A feeling of calm and gratitude washed over me. Now, I was certain that the time had come for me to take the leap of faith and forge the next chapter of my life, on my terms.

The expressions on the faces of my colleagues, as they entered that bus, made me truly thankful that I had listened to my intuition, pursued my dream, and worked my exit plan. On that fateful December day, I had options that my colleagues on the bus did not have. This was a defining moment in my life. While apprehensive about what the future would hold, I was excited by the possibilities. The timing was right to close the door to my life as a corporate citizen. At the same time, a new door opened -- as an author, speaker, executive coach, and business owner. I stepped into the future on my own terms to create the next chapter of my life.

Why is my story relevant to you? It's because it illustrates that with a dream, a plan, and belief in yourself, it is possible to create a future of your own choosing. The greatest ability you will ever have is the ability to live life on your own terms. I am a firm believer that if we do not find ways to control our own destinies, then we become pawns in the hands of those who do. The events of that rainy day in December 2002 illustrate this point on a grand scale.

Workforce reductions, hostile takeovers, acquisitions, and restructurings happen every day. In fact, there is a high probability that you, or someone close to you, either has been, or will be affected by the rapidly changing business environment. Choosing to walk away, as I did, is not an option for everyone. It was an option for me because I had taken the time during the three prior years to develop a plan for my life based on my vision of what I wanted my life to be, and systematically implemented the steps. You can too. Knowing that you have the skills, confidence, and courage to be successful goes a long way in helping you weather the tough times and emerge triumphant.

The fear and anxiety on the faces of the people on that bus is something I will never forget. I took the leap of faith and moved on, knowing that I had done everything I could to prepare myself for the transition. During the difficult times, I use this vision as my inspiration to keep going. Following the steps of Jovita's Success Prescription, described later in this book, prepared me to get out of my own way and pursue my dreams in spite of fear and the obstacles in my path. My prescription provides strategies and insights that can help you realize your dreams as well.

The journey through life is filled with opportunities and challenges. Some people grasp the opportunities and turn challenges into additional opportunities. These are the more successful people. Others struggle, trying to just get through the day, follow the pack, and never lead the charge. What separates the more successful people from everyone else? It is the ability to get out of their own way and keep striving for greatness in spite of the challenges.

This book is a map to help those who want to increase their odds of success. It is a guide to help you chart your course, according to your own definition of success. It chronicles my journey and the lessons I have learned over time, in corporate settings, as a businesswoman, executive coach, and as a person struggling to find my own path through this journey called life. My mission is to provide strategies and tools to help you Get Out Of Your Own Way™ so that you too can design and implement the changes you need to make to create your own compelling future.

CHAPTER TWO

Success Roadblocks

The pearl of great price is the struggle to be true to yourself.

-- Unknown

A re you as successful as you would like to be in all areas of your life? Does your personal definition of success guide your life choices? Are you living your passion? For most of us, the answer to each of these vitally important questions is a resounding no. Somewhere along the path we took down the road of life most of us lost our passion, gave up on our dreams, and conformed to what was expected of us. We have adopted popular definitions of success as our own and live our lives accordingly.

You can be, do, and have anything you want.

But first, you must learn to Get Out Of Your Own Way.

Recall what Get Out Of Your Own Way™ means:

    1. Changing beliefs and behaviors that no longer

serve you

2. Discovering your passion and purpose

3. Setting goals and taking action toward reaching them

4. Overcoming the fear that can hold you back

5. Giving yourself permission to dream, and

6. Implementing the steps to turn your dreams into reality.

Many of us feel stuck, in a rut, unable to move forward. Using the Olympics as a metaphor, when it comes to going for the gold on the road to success in the game of life, we can each be our own worst enemy. Often, we stop ourselves from going for the gold. We block our success by the way we think, and the actions that our thoughts cause us to take (or not take).

Whether we realize it or not, our actions are a function of our internal programming. As children, we start out open to all possibilities. As we learn and grow, we begin to close down based on what we extrapolate from our life circumstances. To get out of the ruts we get ourselves into, we must first understand that our internal programming rules our actions. The first step toward making any significant change is realizing that change is needed. Given that understanding, we can then act to modify our internal programming. This chapter provides the realization piece. Subsequent chapters explore how to change your internal programming using my Prescription.

To go for the gold in the game of life, many of us need to re-program our internal computers -- modify our internal programming. For purposes of this discussion, our internal programming consists of the following elements:

- Social programming
- Belief systems
- Doubt, fear, and guilt
- Self-talk
- Habits
- Defenses

Social Programming

One of the greatest human needs is the need to be

accepted by others of our kind. According to Abraham Maslow, the famous psychologist, only food and shelter rank higher than acceptance in the Hierarchy of Needs. Our parents, teachers, clergymen, employers, and other significant individuals in our lives make sure we know what they consider to be acceptable behavior in any given situation.

When we comply with acceptable behavior, we are rewarded, or at least not punished. When we do not comply, we risk punishment and ostracism from the group. In many cases, we feel guilt and shame when we attempt to accomplish anything that goes against the group norm. The messages we receive are clear: "Don't stand out too much". "Be realistic". These comments in my opinion send a clear message: It's OK to remain mediocre. This is the wrong message, if what you want is to be as successful as you possibly can be at whatever you decide to pursue.

Don't misunderstand my message here. Group norms are necessary in a civilized society. They are the basis for our laws. However, we must keep in mind that norms are established to keep us in line, even when it is not in our best interest. Success in turning your dreams into reality requires independent thinking. Which in turn can require not going along with the crowd or following the group.

We are also programmed by the advertising and entertainment messages we receive. Television, radio, magazines and billboards provide very specific messages about what is acceptable and "in". We receive cultural messages about what we should wear, how we should look, what we should drink, and a myriad of other messages. We are bombarded with advertisements that say youth is everything. That's fine when we are young. However, as we age, we must redefine our image of beauty or feel completely left out. This is particularly true for women.

For those of us that are members of the baby-boom generation, we face another key stumbling block as we strive to make our way and be successful in today's world. Our social programming prepared us to live in an era that no longer exists. For example, we were taught that if you followed the accepted social rules that you could count on a job for life. That social contract no longer exists. We must each be prepared to continuously learn, unlearn, and relearn if we expect to remain viable contributors to society and be able to make a living to support ourselves, and our families.

Even though baby boomers were socialized according to the old rules, now, the social contract, if we can still call it that, is very different. In the workplace, you are only as good as your last success. You must continually prove yourself and demonstrate why you are still the best candidate for a particular job. And you must keep proving it, over and over again. Many of us are not prepared to deal with this reality.

My message is that you must decide on your own path and follow it. Don't let the voices of criticism, what I like to call the "they" voices, keep you on the sidelines. Don't let fear of rejection keep you from going for the gold. There is an old African proverb that says: "The secret to life is to have no fear". Another saying, one that works better for me, is the title of Susan Jeffers book:

"Feel The Fear And Do It Anyway".

It takes courage to follow your own path. Give yourself permission to be brave and do what feels right to you. I am not suggesting that you do anything that is unethical or illegal. I am advocating that you think for yourself and go for what feels right for you. In the end, you are solely responsible for creating a life you love.

Belief Systems

Our belief systems ultimately determine the course of our lives. To a large extent, how successful we are is a function of what we believe we can accomplish. Some beliefs are empowering – they strengthen your foundation and move you to action in the direction you desire. Other beliefs are limiting – they hold you back and leave you feeling disempowered. Have you heard the saying "If you believe you can't, you're right?" You must believe you can accomplish your goal before you can make it happen. There is an expanded discussion on this topic in the next chapter.

Doubt, fear, and guilt

Most roadblocks to success are psychological. As previously stated, we are programmed to act in accordance with what society wants (our social programming). We want to be loved and liked. Once the social program is subliminal, we wind up keeping ourselves in check. It is called being more mature and settled. Deviating from our social programming cause us to feel anxiety, which manifests in the form of doubt, fear, and guilt. In effect, we beat ourselves up. To be able to Get Out Of Your Own Way, you must free your mind of these powerful emotions. Or, you must act, in spite of them (e.g. "Feel the fear and do it anyway").

Self-Talk

You can either be your own best friend, or your own worst enemy. How you talk to yourself can determine whether you remain stuck or move forward toward your goal. If your self -talk includes positive messages, such as "I know I can handle any situation that occurs", then you are more likely to be successful. If instead, you tell yourself to "be realistic" or, ask yourself questions like: "What makes you think you can do that?", then you are doomed to failure before you get started. Pay attention to your self-talk. How you talk to yourself can be a key determining factor in whether or not you are able to reach your goals.

Habits

What is a habit? Simply stated, a habit is a behavior that you keep repeating. It's something you do so often that it becomes easy, sometimes even unconscious. How often do you think about brushing your teeth in the morning? Does your car seem to drive itself to work? Approximately 90% of our normal behavior is based on habits. Our habits determine how our life operates. If we foster good habits, life runs smoothly; if we don't, it doesn't. When your behaviors are in line with your vision, you have a much greater chance of being successful. Periodically, review your habits. By systematically changing just one habit at a time, you can dramatically improve your life.

Defensiveness

Our inner defenses serve a purpose -- they protect us. However, this protection can be a double-edged sword. Defenses help us cope better with life. They keep us from harm in potentially dangerous situations. Defenses can also be major impediments to achieving our goals. They can easily serve as roadblocks by preventing insight into ourselves and others. The key message here is to be more aware of how you use your defenses. Notice whether or not they are helping you, or getting in the way of reaching your objectives.

The traits introduced above provide examples of obstacles you may encounter as you attempt to Get Out of Your Own Way. Be aware of these, as well as numerous other obstacles, as you move forward. In subsequent chapters, strategies are introduced that are designed to help you overcome roadblocks you may encounter on your road to creating your compelling future.

*Criticism is the disapproval
of people, not for having
faults, but for having faults
different from their own.*
                    --Anon

PART II

There is no data on the future.
--Laurel Culter

CHAPTER THREE

Jovita's Success Prescription

Don't just move with the cheese -- redesign the maze!
-- Jovita Jenkins

The road to success is filled with obstacles and bumps. Have you ever wondered why some people seem to always be able to successfully navigate the road, navigate around the obstacles, and safely traverse the bumps? Despite the odds against it, some of us get from where we start out initially to where we want to be, in spite of the challenges we face along the way. And, many of us accomplish this feat not just once, but many times throughout our lives.

There comes a time, though, when no matter how successful we have been in the past, that our success formula no longer works. This phenomenon seems to happen more frequently during the rapidly changing, turbulent times in which we currently live. In fact, strategies that worked last year, or as recently as last week, may have to be modified if we want to continue to be successful in the future.

There are times in most of our lives when we wonder whether or not we have what it takes to be successful. As discussed in the previous chapter, the workplace of the 21st century provides an excellent example. There are no guarantees. Changes in organizational structure, management, or a downturn in the economy can trigger massive layoffs and business reversals.

Or, on the other hand, we may be wildly successful. Human nature is such that we begin to wonder whether we can sustain our success, or whether or not we have what it takes to go to the next level. Changes in our personal lives can also wreak havoc, regardless of whether the change is viewed as good or bad. We get married or divorced. We have children, take on caretaker roles for our parents, or join the empty nesters.

All of these events breed uncertainty about our coping and success skills. It is during the challenging times, when we encounter roadblocks, or have to climb mountains, that we separate the truly successful people from those who fall by the wayside along the side of the road of life.

Early on, in my journey through life, I became a student of what it takes to be successful. I have always been, and continue to be, fascinated with finding out why it is that some people are wildly successful, and some are not able to reach the success levels to which they aspire. Or, even worse, why some people don't aspire to anything other than just "getting by". What I have discovered is that those who feel that they have the greatest control over their futures are consistently more successful than those who don't.

This section of the book (Part II) contains the wisdom I have gained as I traversed my own success paths (yes, there have been several). It incorporates not only my experience, but also the success strategies of my corporate colleagues, business, and coaching clients. The principles are simple, but profound. The strategies can be adapted to fit almost any situation. In the next five chapters, you will be introduced to Jovita's Success

Prescription. I will also share the rational for the prescription, provide action steps for utilizing my prescription, and tips to speed you along your individual paths to success, however you define it. The Prescription elements are:

1. Re-train your brain
2. Discover your passion and purpose
3. Develop your action plan
4. Walk the walk and talk the talk
5. Develop a Dream Team

Redesign the Maze

One of the most talked about business books in the last few years was a little book by Spencer Johnson, entitled "Who Moved My Cheese". The story is a great metaphor for change. It chronicles the escapades of two mice and two little people who live in a maze and look for cheese to nourish them and make them happy. The cheese represents whatever is important to you and the maze represents where you look for the cheese.

As you might expect, one day the characters in the

story arrive in the maze and find the cheese is gone. The mice immediately search for, and find, new cheese. One of the little people reluctantly searches for, and eventually finds new cheese, the other one remains paralyzed by fear and refuses to venture out into the maze. I chose not to identify with any of the characters in the story. My goal is to not just look for new cheese (someone else's cheese), but to re-invent the maze (make my own).

My purpose in introducing you to Jovita's Success Prescription is to provide you with tools and techniques that can help you redefine your maze (success, however you define it). Then, instead of finding the cheese left by someone else, you can decide how to configure the maze and where to put the cheese (your favorite kinds, of course) in it. In short, my goal is to help you determine how to redefine the maze and it's content, not just move with the cheese.

Before you can hit the jackpot, you have to put a coin in the machine.
                              --Flip Wilson

CHAPTER FOUR

Re-Train Your Brain

Yes, you have a gold mine between your ears; your mind and your imagination.

--Earl Nightingale

Have you ever wondered why it is that in spite of your best intentions, you are not able to consistently accomplish the goals and objectives you set for yourself? Most people never reach the heights of success to which they aspire. In fact, most of us are our own worst enemy when it comes to sabotaging our success. One key reason for this is that our internal programming gets in the way.

As discussed in Chapter 2, we are programmed, from birth, to fit in with the community in which we live. Our programming comes from our parents, teachers, religious leaders, politicians, friends, and other groups. The messages we receive are played over and over again in our minds until they become an unconscious part of who we are. To become as successful as we would like to be, we must modify our internal programming. In effect, we must retrain our brains to include new, more empowering beliefs, think new thoughts, form new habits, and take compelling action.

What we believe, the way we think, the words we use, and the habits we acquire, often do not serve us well. Beliefs, thoughts, words, habits, and actions are key factors in determining how successful we are, or may become, regardless of how we define success.

Beliefs are powerful – they color our perceptions of the world around us. And, what are our beliefs designed for? They are the guiding force that drives the generalizations we use to simplify our lives so that we can function in our world. Our beliefs determine what we are able to perceive and ultimately what we are able to achieve. Beliefs have the awesome potential to either create or destroy. They can be empowering or limiting. We will explore this concept later in this chapter.

Thoughts are based on beliefs. Our thoughts have the power to either propel us forward, or hold us back. Our thoughts determine our actions. The words we use to express our thoughts can either be positive and keep us moving forward, or negative, and impede our success.

Our thoughts and beliefs determine our habits, and our habits ultimately determine our future. Bad habits can keep us mired in behaviors that are familiar and comfortable, even when those behaviors no longer support our growth and development. Good habits foster behaviors that help you achieve the success you desire.

Habits determine behavior. Our behavior determines our actions, and our actions determine our results. Getting out of your own way requires retraining your brain so that your beliefs, thoughts, words, and habits are aligned with your vision of who you can become and the goals you want to accomplish.

Relationship Between Beliefs and Actions

Have you ever wondered why in spite of your plans, intentions, and sincere desire to change, you revert to behaviors that can keep you from attaining the goals you set for yourself? We attend seminars, and leave them with the conviction to change our lives. It only takes a few days, and sometimes only a few minutes, to revert to our old ways of functioning. We buy books and tapes designed to help us change some aspects of our lives, our finances, our health and fitness, or our general well being. Our collection of self-help materials increases, but our behaviors remain the same.

Why can't we consistently achieve what we think we should be capable of achieving? Most of us start out enthusiastic about our prospects. We truly intend to change. The problem seems to lie in our inability to sustain our commitment to change. The reason it is so difficult to sustain this commitment is that what we do, feel, and experience is determined by our beliefs – about who we are, what we deserve to accomplish, and how we interact in the world. Fear, limiting and negative beliefs have been programmed into our subconscious and now silently control our actions. Recall that our actions, and ultimately our results, are determined by our beliefs.

The self-help industry thrives because people are searching for ways to stop blocking their success so they can transform their lives and reach their full potential. We are each searching for the magic pill that allows you to Get Out Of Your Own Way™.

Intuitively, I have always known that there was a strong relationship between belief and action. My experiences in corporate America and my interactions with my coaching clients only make this conviction stronger. You must believe in the possibilities, before you can achieve the goal. My underlying belief -- that I create my own reality -- has allowed me to accomplish goals that few people I have known in my life so far could conceive of, much less achieve. And, at mid-life, I have another 30 or so years to create a different reality from the one I experience today. This is also true for each of you reading this book. You get what you focus on, and what you focus on is ultimately determined by your beliefs.

In doing the research for this book, the more I learned about the relationship between beliefs and actions (or lack thereof), the more convinced I became that the key to unlocking your potential lies in your ability to change your beliefs. This includes letting go of beliefs that no longer serve you. It also includes replacing those beliefs with ones that support your continued growth and development in whatever area of your life you choose.

In recent years, quite a lot of attention has been paid to the concept of changing your belief structures so that you can live your best life. This is one of the premises upon which the coaching profession is based. It is also a popular tenet of self-help television shows such as The Oprah Show. Numerous popular authors have written about the power of beliefs to shape your life. The works that come readily to mind are Dr. Phil Shaw's "You'll See It When You Believe It", Anthony Robbins' "Awaken the Giant Within", Lynn Grayhorn's "Excuse Me Your Life Is Waiting", and Morty Lefkoe's "Recreate Your Life". There has also been a considerable amount of study done on this subject in the medical community. The mind/body connection is currently one of the greatest areas of advanced study.

The basic premise is that no matter how committed you are to accomplishing a goal, you will sabotage yourself rather than do something that goes against your basic belief system. It is a fact, that in many cases, our belief systems are invisible to us. And, even though we may not be conscious of our beliefs, we act according to them. Therefore, changing those beliefs that impede your progress is a necessary pre-condition for success.

Empowering vs. disempowering beliefs

Our belief systems ultimately determine the course of our lives. To a large extent, how successful we are is a function of what we believe we can accomplish. Some beliefs are empowering -- they strengthen your foundation and move you to action in the direction you desire. Other beliefs are limiting -- they hold you back and disempower you. In Anthony Robbin's classic book, "Awaken the Giant Within", he states that "beliefs have the awesome potential to create or destroy. ...Learn to choose the beliefs that empower you, create convictions that drive you in the direction of your destiny..."

Survival Strategy Beliefs

Whether we realize it or not, we all devise survival strategy beliefs. Many psychologists call this phenomenon "conditioning". Our survival strategies help us function in the world as we see it. Psychologist, Marty Lefkoe postulates in his book, "Recreate Your Life", that survival strategy beliefs are based on a person's observation of what it takes to feel good about oneself, to be important, worthwhile, or just be able to deal with life. He concludes that "The role of survival strategy beliefs explain why therapies designed only to improve self-esteem rarely produce fundamental and lasting change in people's lives". To make a fundamental life change, you must first change your conditioning or survival strategy beliefs.

Using myself as an example, I developed survival strategies that allowed me to function, and be successful, as a black woman in the male dominated world of the aerospace industry. In that environment, there were daily messages, both overt and covert, that I was not acceptable. My way of surviving, and overcoming the obstacles I faced, was to develop survival strategy beliefs that allowed me to deal with the realities I saw in my professional environment and despite that feel good about myself, and my accomplishments.

The survival strategy beliefs that helped me to succeed in the aerospace industry, did not serve me well when I transitioned out of that environment and into the entrepreneurial world of coaching, speaking, and writing. As an entrepreneur, I had to develop a new set of survival strategies. In fact, the transition required major changes in my thinking and habits so that I could more effectively function in this next phase of my life. No longer could I expect a check on a regular basis. I had to learn to market my services and to recognize opportunity and attract clients and customers. I had to devise new ways of interacting with the world.

There was, however, a ripple effect that I had not anticipated. Devising new ways of interacting with the world is accomplished by trial and error. And some of the errors were very painful. As I developed new ways of interacting in one area of my life, I discovered that some of my prior stable, well established, working relationships were adversely affected. I found out the hard way that any change you make in one area of your life affects other areas of your life in ways you may not be able to anticipate.

Any change in you affects your relationships with the people in your life. The significant others in your life have an established view of who you are and how you should act. When you deviate from that view, you open yourself up to potential conflict at a time when you may be emotionally unable to deal with it effectively. This phenomenon is one reason why people sabotage their success and decide to maintain the status quo. It takes work and lots of good communication to keep your relationships in tact as you change. I can testify that it is worth the effort it takes to successfully (and sometimes painfully) make the transition. However, it took lots of work and communication to maintain the parts of my life that were working fine before my major transition. Hum, maintaining significant relationships while in transition, what a great subject for my next book!

Thoughts

Our thoughts have the power to either propel us forward or hold us back. Changing a single thought can have a significant affect on your ultimate results. Thoughts are like magnets that draw to you what you think about most. Not what you want most, but what you think about most. So, think about what you **want** to happen in your life, not about what you don't want.

What happens when you focus on what you don't want? You attract more of it. According to the Law of Attraction: You attract to your life whatever you give your attention, focus, and energy to, whether wanted or unwanted. For example, I have always envisioned myself as a problem solver. I am really good at solving problems. During my corporate career, one of my roles was to handle the problems that occurred within my organization. So what do you suppose kept showing up? You guessed it, more problems for me to solve. It seemed that as soon as I'd resolve a conflict here, or put out a fire there, a new challenge would surface. My focus was on problems and that is what I got. Now, to the greatest extent possible, I focus on what I want to happen in my life.

The Law of Attraction holds for money, love, or

anything else you might want. In all cases, you attract what you think about, focus on, and give energy to. So if you want love, think loving thoughts. If you want money, think about abundance. Focus on what you want. Stop focusing on what you don't want. I am not naïve enough to think that attraction alone will change your life, and I know you aren't either. The point is focus has power. And, focus combined with action has the potential to change your life.

When you change your thinking about yourself and your possibilities, you attract the forces necessary to turn your thoughts and ideas into real-life experiences. Before you create anything in the physical world, you must first have a thought. You control and determine your future by the thoughts you think in the present.

Exercise

Take out your journal and jot down as many empowering beliefs as you can think of in five minutes. Circle the three most empowering beliefs on your list. How do they empower you? How do they help you in your life? Record your answers in your journal. Next, jot down all the limiting beliefs you can think of. Circle the three most disempowering beliefs on your list. Question yourself about the cost of holding on to these beliefs. Record your answers. Decide to no longer pay the price that these limiting beliefs exact on your life. Finally, identify empowering beliefs to replace the limiting beliefs you want to eliminate. Record these in your journal.

The purpose of this exercise is to provide a mechanism for exchanging limiting beliefs with more powerful empowering beliefs. If you realize, believe, and trust that you can change the meaning and feeling about an event in your mind, you can change your actions. Changing your actions, cause changes in your results.

Passion is spirit jolting, life infusing. It's the fearless, urgent, one-on-one connection between you and a thing, an idea, a talent, or another person.

-- Unknown

CHAPTER FIVE

Discover Your Passion and Purpose

Everyone has a purpose in life... a unique gift or special talent to give to others.

-- Deepak Chopra

D o you loose track of time because you are so caught up in what you are doing that you are not aware of the time passing by? If so, you are doing what you were wired to do -- you are living your passion. Passion gives you a reason to keep going when the going gets tough. Purpose ignites the spirit, creating energy and momentum. Passion and purpose together allow us to unleash the unbridled power to move our lives forward in the direction of our dreams at a faster tempo than ever before.

The problem is that most of us are not living our passion. In fact, in many cases we have no clue where our passions lie. We are so busy just getting through the day that we have no time or energy left to determine what our passions are, much less pursue them vigorously.

Uncovering our passions and finding our purpose takes time and introspection. This chapter provides strategies and questions to help you discover your passion and purpose. To get the most out of the material presented, I recommend that you keep a journal handy. As you go through the material, record your answers to the questions posed and your thoughts. This process can help you gain clarity faster as you strive to uncover your passion and purpose.

Discover your Passion

To discover your passion, you must recognize who you are now, remember who you wanted to be, and decide who you could become. Life is about reinterpreting and revisiting. You have to decide how to spend your days, because in the end, that is how you will have spent your life.

Who are you now?

To begin to get a sense of who you are now, answer the following questions:

Passion --What do you love to do?

1. What activities give you the most satisfaction?
2. What excites you about life?
3. What is your secret ambition?
4. What are your hobbies?

Talents--What are you good at?

1. What do you do better than anyone else?
2. What have other people told you that you are really good at?
3. Where have you excelled in the past?
4. Where have you been successful?
5. What are your major strengths?

Values --What is important to you?

1. What would you do if money were no obstacle?
2. What do you stand for? What won't you stand for?
3. What would you be willing to risk your life for?
4. Given only 1 year to live, how would you spend the time?
5. What values guide your daily life?

Destiny --What were you born to do?

1. What is your unique mission in life?
2. What is the divine purpose for your life?
3. What unique opportunities have been placed in your path?
4. Where can you make a difference?
5. What is your destiny?

Remember who you wanted to become.

As we grow, age, and just live, our view of who we are and what we want changes. The dreams of our youth are not necessarily the same dreams we have now (if we still dream). However, who we wanted to be contains clues to our passions. Answer the following questions. Record the answers in your journal:

1. As a teenager or young adult, what did you want to be when you grew up?
2. Answer the questions in the *"who are you now"* section.

Who do you want to become?

Answer the following questions:

1. What will your life be like in five years if you continue on your current path?

2. Is that the future you want? If not, what are you doing to change direction?

3. What does "success your way" mean to you?

4. What steps are you willing to take to be successful?

Take a few minutes to consider your future. Give yourself permission to dream a **big** dream. Pretend there were no obstacles in your path. What would you dare to dream if you knew it would come true? Now, imagine yourself living from **inside** your dream. Record your vision in your journal for each of the following:

1. Describe your vision. Be as specific as possible.

    *   Where are you?
    *   Who are you with?
    *   Where do you live?

2. Describe your home, including sights, smells, and sounds.

3. Describe your close relationships.

4. Describe your financial situation.

5. Describe the state of your health.

6. Describe your perfect day.

Remember this is a description of your vision for your future. You have the power to turn this dream into reality. Using the strategies in this book, you can create a wonderful new chapter of your life.

Purpose

As mentioned earlier, purpose is the spark that ignites the spirit. People who live their lives with passion and purpose generally like what they do. They also like whom they do it for and/or with, and where they do it. They are healthier and have more nurturing relationships. The classic book, "Repacking your Bags", written by Leider and Shapiro, contains a formula that, in my opinion, appropriately describes living your life with passion and purpose, namely: *(Talents + Passion + Environment) x Vision = Lifestyle Rich in Purpose.*

According to Lieder and Shapiro, "Purpose is not something you have to invent - it's something you discover". You may not be aware of it, or be able to name it, but it's already there. The process detailed in the previous section goes a long way toward helping you discover your passion and your purpose. And, when you discover it, you will find that it has been there all along.

It may take some time to discover your purpose. Unfortunately, for many of us it takes a crisis to discover (or rediscover) our purpose. However, you do not have to wait for a crisis to begin making changes to transform your life. The questions posed in the section on Passion can also help you discover your purpose. The answers to these questions should already be recorded in your journal (assuming you actually answered the questions - if not, answer them now).

Develop Your Personal Purpose Statement

One technique I have found helpful when working with my coaching clients on clarifying and prioritizing their goals is to develop a personal purpose statement.

While compiling the research for this book, I found that one of the best formulas for defining a personal purpose statement comes from the Lieder and Shapiro book mentioned previously. In it they propose that your purpose statement can be compiled from the answers to three questions:

- What are your talents?
- What are you passionate about?
- What environment feels most natural to you?

The answers to these questions should be recorded in your journal.

Illustration

To illustrate the process of developing a personal purpose statement based on the answers to the above questions, I will share with you my current purpose statement (it changes as I learn and grow). Here are my answers to the questions together with my personal purpose statement.

Question 1:

What are your talents?

I am a natural teacher, facilitator, and coach with great intuition

Question 2:

What are you passionate about?

My passion is to help individuals and organizations get out of their own way and reach their peak potential.

Question 3:

What environment feels most comfortable for you? (i.e. In what settings do you feel most comfortable expressing your talents?)

I feel most comfortable expressing myself in writing, in speeches to large groups, and facilitating workshops and seminars in structured settings.

My purpose statement:

My purpose in life is to use my writing, speaking, facilitation, and coaching skills to help individuals and organizations get out of their own way and reach their peak potential.

Exercise

Now, it's your turn, using my example as a model, and your answers to the three questions, devise your own personal purpose statement. Write it down, and post it where you can see it on a regular basis to help you stay focused.

*Good plans shape good decisions.
That's why good planning helps
to make elusive dreams come true.
--Lester R. Bittel*

Develop Your Action Plan

One step in the right direction is worth a hundred years of thinking about it.   *– T. Harve Eker*

Getting out of your own way requires action planning. A key distinguishing attribute of successful people is that they focus on their significant goals and develop plans of action to achieve them. Your plan of action may change over time, as you gain new information and insight. Your goal may change as well. As you acquire more knowledge you may decide on a different direction. That's OK. You need a way to get started. So flex your decision-making muscles and pick a goal, develop a plan, and start working it. If you keep doing what you have always done, you will keep getting the results that you have always gotten. If you want to change your life, you must take action. This chapter is devoted to helping you develop action plans.

A well conceived action plan answers the

following questions:

Where am I now?

Where am I going?

What do I need to get there?

What route can I take to get there?

What can I do to reward myself for progress at key milestones?

Plans that work have several common features:

- They are objective
- They are future focused
- They are simple, yet complete
- They are flexible so you can change them if circumstances warrant.

Two methods for identifying action steps to incorporate in your plan immediately come to mind: the brainstorming method and the back step method.

Brainstorming method

This method requires asking "What if" questions. Think of all the possible obstacles, challenges, and opportunities. Imagine dealing successfully with each one. Visualize the plan. Write down the steps. Begin implementing them.

Back Step Method

Picture your goal. Imagine that you have already achieved it. Then pretend you are looking back from the position of having achieved your goal to determine the steps that got you there. Ask yourself, what steps you took just before you reached your goal. Then ask yourself what step you took just before that. Work backwards until you get to where you are now. Fill in as many steps as you can. Then, get started working toward the first step (starting from where you are now). As you accomplish each step, review your overall plan. Make adjustments if necessary, but keep moving forward.

Measure your progress.

It is important to know how you are doing on your path to attaining a goal. Ask yourself the following questions:

What are your criteria for success?

How do the results of your plan measure against the objectives you have set?

It is important to know when to continue, change direction, or stop and try something new. Monitor your progress. As you move along your path toward success, you may encounter roadblocks. You may also discover that the direction in which you are moving is no longer the one you want to take. Don't be afraid to change course when necessary. Reassess your position periodically. Change course when necessary. Find ways to reward yourself for your effort along the way. There are many attractive parking spaces on the road to success. Don't park along the curb. Finish the race!

Goals

You translate your dreams into concrete reality by turning them into goals. Decide what you want. Write them down. There is something about writing it down that makes it more concrete. I can't explain why, but it works. It's like your subconscious begins to identify ways to turn the goal into a reality. In fact, keep a goal journal. Write down all of the goals you would like to accomplish in the journal. Add to it as often as you like. Review the journal regularly. Set a deadline for each goal. Determine what you have to do to achieve it. So what if the deadline or action steps you select is a WAG (Wild Ass Guess). It helps to get your brain focused on what you want and start working on ways to achieve it.

Don't think of your goals, think from your goals. What do I mean by that? Visualize yourself having accomplished your goals. Where do you live? Who are you with? What is the view from your office or living room window? Think from that place. Whatever is meaningful to you. -- think from there. That thought gives you power.

I recall the first time I looked out of the window of a high-rise office building in Century City. I knew that was where I wanted my company's office to be. High up enough to see the mountains and the office towers. That view gave me the kick I needed to go get more business so that I could afford the space I wanted. I saw myself there every time I had a client interaction or a discussion with a potential client.

What inspires you? What do you want to do? What vision of your future gives you the kick you need to get out there and make it happen?

Always ask yourself these
two questions to turn failure
into success:
"What did I do right?"
"What would I do differently?"

Ability is what you're capable of doing. Motivation determines what you do. Attitude determines how well you do it.

--Lou Holtz

Walk-The-Walk and Talk-The-Talk

All that is necessary to break the spell of inertia and frustration is this: act as if it were impossible to fail.
                                        --Dorothea Brande

Taking the first step on any journey can be the hardest one. We want to start at the right time, or in the right place, or with the right set of conditions. And, we usually view the right time, place, and conditions as occurring sometime in the future, never right now. Given this tendency, it is not surprising that many of us never start the journey and consequently never reach our peak potential.

The goal of this chapter is to help kick-start you into action. There is a saying I'd like to share with you that provides a great visual to help motivate me when I feel stuck. I use this saying to help kick-start myself into action: "For many people, life is a search for a proper manila envelope in which to get themselves filed". The thought of getting myself filed in a manila folder is not my idea of success. And, if you have gotten to this point in my book, I assume it is not your idea of success either.

I want to live on the outer edge of my potential, not on the inner edge of my security. How about you? Do you want to live on the outer edge of your potential and create a fulfilling and satisfying life? Or, would you prefer to live on the inner edge of your security, play it safe, and never reach your peak potential? The choice is yours.

Getting started down any path that is unfamiliar requires that you be willing to step out of your comfort zone. Stepping into unknown territory opens you up to the possibility of failure. Fear of failure has kept many a person paralyzed, unable to move in the direction of their goals. But keep in mind, that if you never risk failure, you guarantee it. You must feel the fear and keep going. Remember, if you keep doing what you have always done, you will keep getting the results that you have always gotten.

To move in new directions, we must unlearn our old way, let go of behaviors that no longer serve us, and learn a new way. Walk-the-walk and talk-the-talk focuses on behavioral change (getting out of your own way). In this chapter, we will introduce the concepts of visualization and actualization as mechanisms for retraining your brain to think differently about your life and your possibilities.

Changing just one behavior can be the catalyst that propels you to new heights of success. Using the techniques described in this chapter can help you change your behavior by:

1. Increasing your level of awareness
2. Increasing your practical understanding of the circumstances and environment
3. Increasing your ability to make good decisions based on knowledge.

Walk-the-walk and talk-the-talk means thinking and acting in new ways for the express purpose of moving you toward your goals. The thoughts conveyed in this chapter are not new. Intuitively we all know that you must be able to picture yourself doing, being, and having what you want before you can make it happen. As previously mentioned, psychological studies have shown that our subconscious mind cannot tell the difference between what we imagine and reality. Therefore, we have the ability to train our brains to accept a new reality, in many cases, before we accomplish the goal.

Visualization and Actualization

We have all heard the sayings "Fake it until you make it" and "act confident before you feel confident". I'd like to add another saying that I think is very appropriate in this context. That saying is: "Practice the future". You practice by vividly visualizing yourself accomplishing the goal – visualization -- and acting as if you had already attained it -- actualization.

Visualization helps you strengthen your resolve to attain your goals. If you can believe it, you can be it. Vivid visualization involves all of your senses. You not only see yourself having accomplished the goal, but you develop a mental picture of where you are, who is with you. You also visualize the sights, sounds, and smells associated with the accomplishment. An example can help make this concept clearer.

Let's say you want to buy a new house. Vividly visualize the house. How many rooms does it have? What color are the walls in each room? How is each room furnished? Who lives there with you? What do you see from the living room window? What smells are coming from the kitchen? Make the visualization as real as possible. Experience the house from the inside. Write down the details in your journal. Revisit this vision on a regular basis. Being able to see yourself in the house helps to motivate you both consciously and at a subconscious level to find ways to make it a reality.

Actualization helps you practice the future. Whenever we assume a new role, we have to figure out what is expected of us. How do we act that is appropriate for the role? We may lack confidence in our ability to do what is expected. A great rule of thumb is to act confident before you feel confident. If you act confident, over time, your brain gets the message and confidence kicks in.

As an aside, men are better at actualization than

women. Men have no problem with WAGs. What are WAGs? They are wild ass guesses! Men will guess and act truly confident, while women have a tendency to want to have all the answers before they act. I know I have been guilty of this. In my opinion, this is one skill that women in the business world need to acquire. Being able to act confident, when you really aren't makes the confidence kick in faster.

What is your dream? What are you visualizing to keep your dream alive? What steps can you take to actualize your dream – practice the future? Here is a tip. When beginning your journey to achieving your goals, focus your early efforts on achieving a few quick successes. Use your early successes to build your confidence in taking the next steps. Remember that many small steps have brought you to where you are now. Keep going, one step at a time. Keep your vision vivid in your mind's eye. Act as if you have accomplished your goal. Find a way to celebrate each success.

Food for Thought

As Strom Thurmond, the longest serving and oldest politician, both in the Republican Party and in the Senate of the United States, neared his 100th birthday, a reporter asked him a question. The question dealt with what he thought was the greatest thing he could think of about becoming 100 years old. The Senator thought for a moment, and then replied, "There is very little peer pressure". It seems even peer pressure, the favorite explanations given for the behavior of young people, can be overcome if one lives long enough.

Maslow, in his hierarchy of needs theory, says that there are five (5) levels that need to be achieved in order for a person to reach the pinnacle of one's true self, that point called self-actualization. Intrinsically, one needs to have these elements at equilibrium within themselves. On the bottom of this pyramid, one needs to understand first and foremost that their survival is not at stake. Their food shelter, air, clothing, the necessities of life are there. Secondly they need to feel safe and secure in their environment. There is a need as social animals for social acceptance, recognition and achievement. The fourth has to do with positive self-esteem. On this base rests the ultimate degree of personal, professional, and other success. That is the point of self-actualization; the point of becoming. That is something all of us go through without question.

It brings me to what I have coined as Jovita's Theory of Extremes. The theory says it doesn't matter where you are on the spectrum of life. It simply matters what you do. Let me give you an example of what I mean by the theory of extremes. We have of course seen genius come from broken single parent, poor, minority, female, etc. families. On the other hand, we have seen, coming from a level of wealth and privilege, morons, criminals, psychopaths, etc., all from seemingly ideal environments. The strata of society in which one is born does not necessarily predict that person's destiny.

Now we have talked about some of the kinds of things that I would call the ingredients of our lives that result in the gumbo, the soup, that we become. What do we do about it? We have talked about the things that make us and that interfere with us -- our beliefs, our procrastinations, and our foibles. What we have learned, is that whatever we want to become, we have to see ourselves as that thing. Feel it, act it, taste it, want it. It is pure folly to under-estimate the power of passion and desire in achieving a goal or reaching an objective. What it takes is what I call CSPAN, which is a survey/plan/act success model.

C – Consciousness

Identify a trait/habit/aspect of your life that you want to change. Denial is no longer an option.

S – Survey/study/explore

Identify new possibilities and alternative actions.

P – Plan

Develop an action plan to implement the change.

A – Action

Implement/modify the steps in the plan as appropriate.

N – Next chapter

Live a more fulfilling/satisfying/joyful life.

TEAM is an acronym that means
Together Everyone Achieves
Miracles.

-- Mark Victor Hansen

CHAPTER EIGHT

Develop A Dream Team

You can accomplish anything with a dream, a plan, and a team.

-- Jovita Jenkins

No one succeeds alone. Having the right team can make the difference between wild success and dismal failure. But don't take my word for it. One of the most read books of all time is Napolean Hill's "Think and Grow Rich". If you haven't read this book yet, you should. In it he espouses fifteen principles that successful people share. Five of these principles are particularly relevant to getting out of your own way:

1. You must have a burning desire

2. You must have faith

3. You must develop a plan

4. You must become decisive in nature

5. You must surround yourself with a mastermind team

This chapter expands on the concept of a mastermind team. According to Hill, the 'Master Mind' is defined as: "Coordination of knowledge and effort, in a spirit of harmony, between two or more people, for the attainment of a definite purpose". In the text he espoused the concept of one plus one equals eleven – not two. Also, in this classic work, Napolean Hill has the distinction of being the first to coin the phrase, "Dream Team".

What is a Dream Team?

A Dream Team is a group of like-minded, success-oriented people focused on helping the team members achieve their individual or collective goals. With the right dream and the right team you can accomplish anything. A wonderful description of a Dream Team is provided in the book, "One Minute Millionaire" by Mark Victor Hansen and Robert Allen. The specific quote is: "Together everyone accomplishes miracles".

With a Dream Team, you create synergy – the sum of the parts is far greater than the whole. People working together, in harmony, leverage the ability of all the members and of a "higher power". According to Hill, 'dream teaming' occurs when two or more individuals come together in the spirit of harmony to accomplish some goal, activity, or result.

The right Dream Team can help you identify and change habits that could hinder your success. The team can identify or provide resources that can help you achieve your goals. I credit my dream with giving me the courage to step out on faith and create the next chapter of my life outside of the corporate umbrella. In turn, each of my Dream Team members have also stepped out and created new realities for themselves that would not have been possible without the input and support of the other team members. Together we are creating an information empire focused on helping individuals, teams, and organizations reach their peak potential.

Dream Teams can also include virtual members. People you admire or people who have accomplished goals you aspire to accomplish. These can be role models and mentors or even people you read about in books. Who are your mentors, your role models? Who are the people you admire the most? What have these people accomplished that makes you respect them so much? Are they doing or have they done what you want to do? The answers to these questions can help select the right members for your Dream Team, which can in turn accelerate your growth from where you are now to where you want to be.

A good coach can also serve as a mentor or member of your Dream Team. The coach's function is to focus on your goals and aspirations, help you plan your strategies for implementation, and keep you accountable to yourself for accomplishing your goals.

How do you select Dream Team members?

Select the members of your Dream Team carefully. A critical success element for a Dream Team is that it contains like-minded members with positive attitudes. Make sure the members are aligned with your vision and values. Choose enthusiastic people with big potential futures who also want to grow. Avoid negative people or people with no vision, as they will hinder the group's progress. Also avoid individuals who are not willing to share resources with the rest of the group.

The Dream Team functions like an extended family. Consequently, all members of the existing group must accept new members unanimously. When considering establishing a new Dream Team, here are a number of questions you should ask to determine if a person is right for your particular group:

- Who are the people who stand in your corner during your most difficult moments?
- What friends have risked telling you the hard truth with grace and love, simply because they care about you?
- Which of your friends refuses to belittle or tear down others, even when those people are not around?
- Who holds you accountable for what you say you are going to do?
- With whom do you feel absolutely safe?

We all need support of some sort to make our dreams a reality. As previously stated, no one succeeds alone. Incredible power is unleashed when people work together for a common goal. Use the criteria above to start building your Dream Team. Use their expertise to help you attain your goals, while also helping your Dream Team members attain theirs. Always remember the saying 'TEAM is an acronym for together everyone achieves miracles".

PART III

*Live on the outer edge of
your potential, not on the
inner edge of your security.
-- Unknown*

CHAPTER NINE

Pulling It All Together

If you want to know what is in your way, look in the mirror.

-- Unknown

We have covered an incredible amount of material in the previous chapters. Part I identified the typical roadblocks we face on our journey through life. Part II introduced the elements of Jovita's Success Prescription, and provided the rationale for using it to help you Get Out Of Your Own Way™. Part III, which begins with this chapter, deals with practical application of my success prescription. In this chapter, the focus is on pulling the pieces together to make the prescription work for you.

A great metaphor for pulling it all together is diagnosing, and then curing, a disease. In the early chapters (Part I), we paint a picture of people who are having difficulty because they are getting in their own way (the disease). The reasons for this are numerous, and for the most part, operate on an unconscious level. The objective was to diagnose the problem -- to make the invisible, visible. To that end, we exposed the social programming that is designed to keep us stuck and going along with the program, whatever that happens to be. The medicine prescribed to help us overcome the disease is Jovita's Success Prescription (Part II). We uncovered and diagnosed the problem and provided the prescription that could provide relief. The last piece is actually taking the medicine (Part III). Implementing the elements of the prescription is equated to taking the medicine required to solve the problem.

The solutions fall into 3 categories: self, relationships, and prosperity. You must decide for yourself, where your main core problem lies. Is it with my self? Are my beliefs and thoughts getting in the way of achieving my goals? Is it with the relationships I am involved in? Are they good, positive? If not, what am I going to do? Is it with my level of prosperity? Do I need more education, to get a better job, or change my spending and saving habits? Each of us must decide what is most important, given our particular situation. Until you decide, nothing will work. Once you decide where you need to start, your potential for growth is limitless. The questions we as ourselves, determine the priorities we set to try to heal ourselves. The questions we ask ourselves help us determine where we start, where we need help the most.

How do you Get Out Of Your Own Way? How do you know what way to get out of? It's by asking yourself the right questions. There must be a reckoning with ourselves to help us cure the patient – us. If we are committed to making that change, we have to decide what to do about it. We can all identify things we would like to change in our lives. A key stumbling block, though, is that sometimes we have trouble determining where to start, or how to establish priorities if there is more than one area requiring our attention. In many cases, this keeps us stuck.

Read this chapter with your journal handy. Capture the answers to the questions posed. Also, capture any thoughts that occur to you. The information you gleam from reflecting on your thoughts and feelings will be extremely beneficial in helping you implement my Get Out Of Your Own Way prescription.

Key Focus Areas

In my experience with coaching clients, there is a recurring theme. With the competing priorities each of us face, where do we start? If you are facing the same dilemma, the following analysis can help you identify a place to start that is relevant to your individual situation.

In analyzing our lives, three key areas come to mind with respect to getting out of your own way:

- Self
- The relationships we are involved in, and
- The prosperity, or lack thereof, in our lives

Which of these areas would provide the greatest benefit to your life if you were to select it as the place to begin -- self, relationships, or prosperity?

What did you take away from the previous chapters? What was your greatest "ah-ha" in terms of learning about what gets in your way? Consider the following:

If we learn that our difficulty is in the way we were acculturated or socialized, and that those belief systems interfere with our ability to get out of our way, then begin here. If our cure lies in changing ourselves emotionally, or spiritually, or in other ways that will foster the healing we need that will enable us to get out of our way, then that is where we begin.

If we determine, based on what we have learned in previous chapters, that our true difficulty lies in the relationships that we have entered into, then we must set relationships as a high priority. We must change those relationships in the ways we need to, or form others.

Finally, if prosperity, or the lack of it, is where our difficulties lie, then we need to prioritize ways of overcoming that. If our difficulties with prosperity need to be met by saving more or investing more or spending more wisely, then that should be our goal for getting out of our way. If our analysis of our state of prosperity suggests that we should be more sharing, then we need to find ways of contributing more and doing other things that we can do to become whole.

Focus Questions

The remainder of this chapter provides questions that can help you get focused and clear on your personal strategy for implementing the changes you need to Get Out Of Your Own Way. The goal here is to help you get really clear on your vision, particularly as it pertains to the focus areas identified above -- self, relationships, and prosperity. Where are you now? Where do you want to go?

The questions posed are designed to help you paint an ideal picture for your life and begin living it today. The goal is to help you focus on what you want -- get really clear. Recall, what you focus on expands. So, focus on what you want, not what you don't want. Then, begin practicing your future!

Recall that we each view our lives from three major perspectives:

- Self
- Relationships
- Prosperity

Everything we deal with, on a daily basis, falls into these three categories. Becoming really clear with respect to our aspirations, intentions, choices, and actions in these areas is key to getting out of your own way. Intuitively, the area that resonates most with you after completing the process, defined below, is the ideal starting place for you.

Start by asking yourself the following introspective questions and writing down the answers:

1. What are my highest aspirations?
2. Who do I want to be?
3. What do I want to do?
4. What do I want to have?

Answer the questions first as it relates to you, the individual (self). Next, answer them as it relates to your relationships, both personal and professional. Finally, answer them from the perspective of prosperity.

Self

Your self is the primary consideration (or at least it should be). The following questions provide the context in which to picture yourself, both today, and, as you see yourself in the future. What are your highest aspirations in relation to your self-image? Are you as physically fit as you would like to be? Mentally are you getting the amount of stimulation you require? Are you expanding your knowledge base in areas of interest to you? What are the states of your emotional, psychological, and spiritual well-being? Are you satisfied with your career, business, and/or work life? Do you enjoy a peaceful, nurturing, aesthetically pleasing environment?

Relationships

Next, your relationships affect how you behave, and the results you get based on your interaction with others. The questions in this section provide the context for valuing the quality of your relationships. Do you enjoy a loving, respectful, supportive, mutually fulfilling relationship with your spouse or significant other? How about with your children or other family members? Do you have quality relationships at work with your peers, subordinates, and managers? If not, which relationships would you change? In what ways would you like to change them?

Prosperity

Finally, your prosperity depends on numerous factors. In particular, it is a function of how you see yourself within your world – as a player, or a pawn. Yes, circumstances are a factor. However, I truly believe that your view of yourself within your environment can make all the difference. Your self-view affects the relationships you establish, and the choices you make. The questions to consider, when assessing your well being with respect to prosperity, include: Am I satisfied with my level of income, investments, and savings? Where am I spending my money? Is it going to increase my well being and prosperity, or am I just getting by? What is the level of my debt? Am I contributing to the causes that are important to me?

Develop your plan

If you have done the work and answered the questions in this chapter, you now have a clearer picture of where you want to go. You also have a clearer picture of how to get started on your path. Develop you plan using the planning information from Chapter 6. If you implement the steps of Jovita's Success Prescription now that you have a clearer picture of how to get from where you are to where you want to be, your potential for success is significantly greater. Begin today, and never give up!

*Live life without fear, confront
all obstacles, and know that
you can overcome them.*
                    -- Unknown

CHAPTER TEN

A New Journey Begins

Two roads diverged in a wood, and I –
I took the one less traveled by,
And that has made all the difference.
-- Robert Frost

I am a firm believer that you have the power to create your own destiny. The Robert Frost poem, "The Road Less Traveled", included above, captures, in just a few words, the essence of this book. You have a choice. You can choose to follow the well-worn path. You can sit around and make excuses for why your life is not going the way you dreamed it would. Or, you have the option to create your own path -- Get Out Of Your Own Way™ and start to make things happen! Choose your path! A wise man once said that the journey of a thousand miles begins with the first step. Congratulations! If you have gotten this far in the book and followed the strategies and advice, you have taken the first step.

To make a change that is lasting, you must consistently do the following four things:

1. Raise your standards. Change what you demand of yourself. Determine all the things you will

   - no longer accept in your life,
   - no longer tolerate, and
   - aspire to become

2. Retrain your brain to eliminate your limiting beliefs – Our beliefs are like unquestioned commands that tell us how things are, what is possible and what is impossible, and ultimately what we can and cannot do. If you don't eliminate you limiting beliefs, you can raise your standards as much as you like, but you will never have the conviction to back them up.

3. Change your strategy – you need the best strategies for achieving results. Follow through using the strategies described in Jovita's Success Prescription.

4. Take action! Taking action is, in effect, what Get Out Of Your Own Way™ is all about. Lots of people **know** what to do, but few people actually **do** what they know. Knowing is not enough. **You have to take**

action. Continually ask yourself the question "What action do I have to take today, in order to create the tomorrow I want to happen"? And, keep telling yourself: "I can handle any situation that presents itself".

Final Thoughts

There are no impossible dreams; just our limited perception of what is possible. If you believe it, you can achieve it! You have the ability to change your life and create the future you desire. My sincere wish is that you utilize the tools and strategies presented in these pages to embark on a new journey -- on the road to the destiny you choose. I'd love to hear about your successes. Keep me informed. Send email to info@jovitajenkins.com. Never forget, your future begins with what you do today to make tomorrow happen. Begin the journey now! GO FORTH, AND CONQUER!

I am, at last, marching to my own drum, connected to what I love most. And, I am 100% committed to the directions I am now taking. Frankly, that is all that matters.

-- Jovita Jenkins

Bibliography

Adrienne, Carol. *Find Your Purpose, Change Your Life*. New York: Quill, 1999.

Beard, Lee and E., Steven. *Wake Up Live the Life You Love*. Laguna Beach, CA: Little Seed Publishing Co., 2003

Canfield, Jack, Mark Victor Hansen and Les Hewitt. *The Power of Focus*. Deerfield Beach, FL: Health Communications, Inc., 2000.

Chopra, Deepak. *The Seven Laws of Spiritual Success*. San Rafael, CA: Amber-Allen Publishing and New World Library, 1994.

Coleman-Willis, Linda. *Loving Yourself First*. Inglewood California: WLW Publishing, 1997.

Covey, Stephen. *The Seven Habits of Highly Effective People*. New York: Simon & Schuster, 1990.

Dyer, Wayne W. *You'll See It When You Believe It*. New York: Harper Collins, 1989.

Ford, Debbie. *The Dark Side of the Light Chasers*. New York: Riverhead Books, 1998.

Fortgang, Laura Berman. *Living Your Best Life*. New York: Jeremy P. Tarcher/Putnam, 2001.

Fortgang, Laura Berman. *Take Yourself to the Top*. New York: Warner Books, 1998.

Foster, Jylla Moore. *Due North! Strengthen Your Leadership Assets*. Hinsdale, IL: Crystal Stairs Publishers, 2002.

Grabhorn, Lynn. *Excuse Me, Your Life Is Waiting*. New York: Hampton Roads Publishing Co.

Hall, Stacey and Jan Brogniez. *Attracting Perfect Customers*. San Francisco, CA: Berrett-Koehler Publishers, Inc., 2001.

Hansen, Mark Victor and Robert G. Allen. *The One Minute Millionaire*. New York: Harmony Books, 2002.

Harrell, Keith. *Attitude is Everything*. New York: Harper Collins, 2000.

Hill, Napoleon. *Think and Grow Rich*. New York: Fawcett Books, 1990.

Hudson, Frederic M. and McLean, Pamela D. *LifeLaunch*. Santa Barbara: The Hudson Institute Press, 2000.

Jeffers, Susan. *Feel the Fear and Do It Anyway*. NewYork: Ballantine Books, 1987.

Johnson, M.D., Spencer. *Who Moved My Cheese?* New York: G.P. Putnam's Sons, 1998.

Kimbro, Dennis P. *What Makes the Great Great: Strategies for Extraordinary Achievement*. New York: Doubleday Books, 1998.

King, Barbara. *Transform Your Life*. New York: Perigee Books, 1995.

Lefkoe, Morty. *Re-Create Your Life*. Kansas City: Andrews and McMeel, 1997.

McGraw, Phillip. *Life Strategies*. New York: Hyperion, 2000.

McGraw, Phillip. *Self Matters*. New York: Simon & Schuster Source, 2001.

Peale, Norman Vincent. *Power of Positive Thinking*. New York: Ballantine Books, 1996.

Pederson, Rena. *What's Next? Women Redefining Their Dreams in the Prime of Life*. New York: Perigee Books, 2001.

Richardson, Cheryl. *Stand Up for Your Life*. New York: The Free Press, 2002.

Richardson, Cheryl. *Take Time for Your Life*. New York: Broadway Books, 1999.

Robbins, Anthony. *Awaken The Giant Within*. New York: Fireside, 1991.

Scott, Susan. *Fierce Conversations*. New York: Viking Penguin, 2002.

Tracy, Brian. *Change Your Thinking, Change Your Life*. Hoboken, NJ: John Wiley & Sons, Inc., 2003.

Von Oech, Roger, *A Whack on the Side of the Head*. New York: Warner Books, Inc., 1990

CPSIA information can be obtained
at www.ICGtesting.com
Printed in the USA
FSHW011228160719
60070FS